It Was Time

info@familytree.pub

Author Pamela Robbins
Contributor Kay Littlejohn
Book design by Eduardo Paj

Paperback ISBN: 978-1-957308-19-7
Library of Congress Control Number: 2022911758

https://familytree.pub

IT WAS TIME

Written by Pamela Robbins

Illustrated by Eduardo Paj

To our future and the people who continue to work
to preserve and enhance the pollination cycle for us all.

The chill of winter lingered over all the land.
When spring insisted - it was time.

It was time for sleeping buds to awake.
It was time for fall's seeds to take root.

With a burst of energy,
color appeared everywhere.
Winter hues exchanged
for a breath-taking array.

The giant Saguaro wore
a crown of blooms.
The Fireweed and Lady Slipper
waved boldly, as Coral Bean
and SpiderLily spread gently.

The call had been heard, and the cycle began.
As the caterpillars ate and the chrysalises
grew, the unwrapping began.

It was time to unwrap the Painted Lady
and Duskywing.
It was time to unwrap the Monarch
Longtail Skipper, and Pearl Crescent.

Emerging slowly, they paused
to dry their delicate wings.

So much to do, so many flowers to visit,
they knew their vital part in this cycle.

With a whisper of wings,
they carried aloft clinging pollen.
For without these carriers,
many plants would not survive.

As the meadows
began to warm,
Honeybee hives stirred,
Carpenter bees and Bumblebees
awoke from hibernation.

They knew their part, too.
It was time to build new hives.
It was time to gather food for their nests.

With a blur of buzzing wings,
they followed the signals.

They found the hidden hollows;
their urgent task clear.

Their job among the petals was important.
They must drink the nectar to feed the hive,
and carry life's pollen dust
from anther to stigma.

Across prairies, along river beds, and on mountain sides,
blossoms waited for a visit from nature's messengers.

The task was simple, yet the act essential.
It was time to share pollen.
It was time for new fruits and seeds.

Once the cycle of spring evolving into summer had begun,
birds joined with the butterflies;
busy ants kept pace with the bees.

The day and night flyers, the crawlers and curious,
each had a job.

There was enough for all to do,
and everyone played their part.

The Honeybee hives began to fill with new life,
as the combs and cells dripped honey.

Summer blooms had attracted a spectrum of wings,
so now…

It was time to watch the flowers close.
It was time to marvel at what replaced the petals.

Soon wild flowers announced the shortening days.
The Foxglove, Paintbrush, and Trillium lingered.

With their work nearly done, the cycle moved on.
Hot winds cooled, as sun shadows lengthened.
Fruits bent the branches; seed pods waited to fall.

As the seasons reliably ushered in change,
the pollination cycle renewed
everything around them.

Fall's preparations were made
so it may begin again.

It was time to seek warmth in the hives.
It was time for next spring's eggs
to be hidden under leaves.

The calm of winter, the cloak of chill,
the slanting rays,
all worked together with the lives of pollinators
who await their turn until...once again...

It was time!

Pollinators:
We Can't Live Without Them
We need them to eat!

Almost all the plants grown
for food around the
world need to be pollinated by animals.

Plants need them to renew!

Animals that pollinate the flowers
and plants make it possible
for those plants to continue to make
more plants next year.

Find out more:

US Department of Agriculture
https://www.fs.usda.gov/managing-
land/wildflowers/pollinators/what-is-pollination
Smithsonian Gardens:
https://gardens.si.edu/gardens/pollinator-garden/why-
what-when-where-who-how-pollination/

About the Author

Dr. Pamela Hallmark Robbins
is an award-winning author
and educator, specializing in literacy
development, reading intervention
strategies and educational leadership.

Pam takes her inspiration
from nature, real-life events,
observations, and the people
she encounters

About the illustrator

Eduardo Paj is an illustrator and graphic
designer. Over the years he has illustrated
numerous award-winning children's books,
computer games, and comics.

Eduardo's images are full of life, rich in color,
and designed with his unique style.
He shares his passion with his lovely
wife and two sons.

www.ingramcontent.com/pod-product-compliance
Lightning Source LLC
Chambersburg PA
CBHW061150030426
42335CB00003B/170